Prison Camps in the Civil War

Untold History of the Civil War

CHELSEA HOUSE PUBLISHERS

Untold History of the Civil War

Prison Camps in the Civil War

Douglas J. Savage

CHELSEA HOUSE PUBLISHERS
Philadelphia

Produced by Combined Publishing
P.O. Box 307, Conshohocken, Pennsylvania 19428
1-800-418-6065
E-mail: combined@combinedpublishing.com
web: www.combinedpublishing.com

CHELSEA HOUSE PUBLISHERS

Editor in Chief: Stephen Reginald
Managing Editor: James D. Gallagher
Production Manager: Pamela Loos
Art Director: Sara Davis
Director of Photography: Judy L. Hasday
Senior Production Editor: LeeAnne Gelletly
Assistant Editor: Anne Hill

Front Cover Illustration: Andersonville prison drawn by Civil War prisoner Thomas
O'Dea. Courtesy of the National Park Service.

The Chelsea House World Wide Website address is
http://www.chelseahouse.com

 35798642

Library of Congress Cataloging-in-Publication Data applied for:
ISBN 0-7910-5428-4

Contents

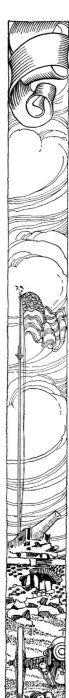

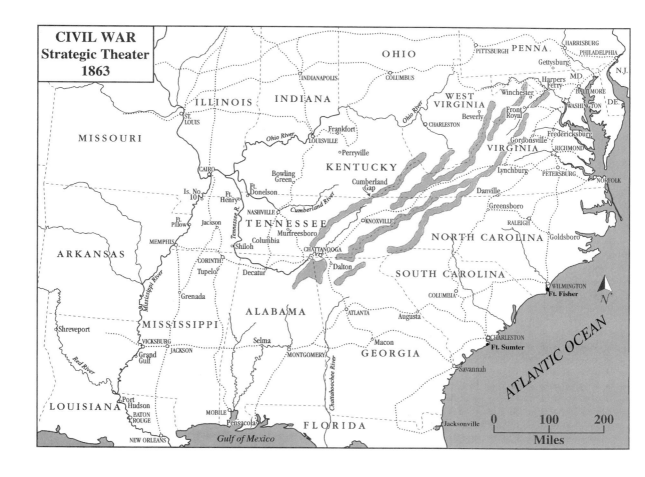

CIVIL WAR Strategic Theater 1863

OHIO

PENNA.

HARRISBURG

PITTSBURGH

Gettysburg

PHILADELPHIA

INDIANAPOLIS

COLUMBUS

WEST VIRGINIA

Winchester

Harpers Ferry

MD.

BALTIMORE

N.J.

DE.

ILLINOIS

INDIANA

Ohio River

Beverly

CHARLESTON

Front Royal

WASHINGTON

MISSOURI

Ohio River

Frankfort

LOUISVILLE

Gordonsville

VIRGINIA

Fredericksburg

RICHMOND

ST. LOUIS

Perryville

KENTUCKY

Lynchburg

PETERSBURG

NORFOLK

CAIRO

Bowling Green

Cumberland Gap

Danville

Is. No. 10

Ft. Donelson

Greensboro

Ft. Henry

Cumberland River

KNOXVILLE

RALEIGH

Ft. Pillow

NASHVILLE

Tennessee R.

Jackson

TENNESSEE

NORTH CAROLINA

Goldsboro

MEMPHIS

Columbia

Murfreesboro

Shiloh

CHATTANOOGA

ARKANSAS

CORINTH

Dalton

SOUTH CAROLINA

Tupelo

Decatur

Grenada

ALABAMA

ATLANTA

COLUMBIA

Augusta

WILMINGTON

Ft. Fisher

N

MISSISSIPPI

Selma

Macon

GEORGIA

CHARLESTON

Ft. Sumter

Shreveport

VICKSBURG

JACKSON

MONTGOMERY

Chattahoochee River

ATLANTIC OCEAN

Grand Gulf

Red River

Savannah

Mississippi River

LOUISIANA

Port Hudson

BATON ROUGE

MOBILE

FLORIDA

Jacksonville

0   100   200

NEW ORLEANS

Pensacola

Gulf of Mexico

Miles

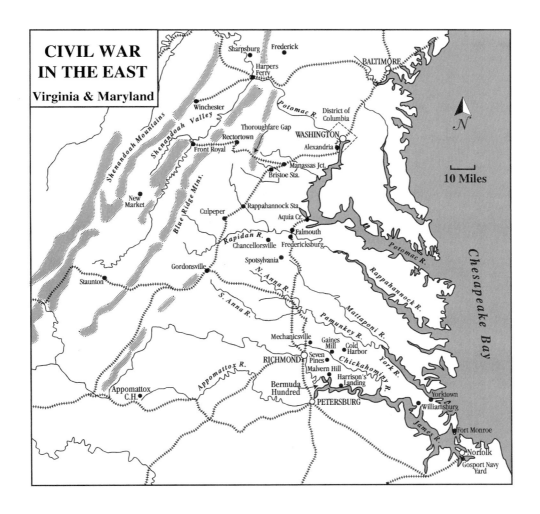

CIVIL WAR
IN THE EAST
Virginia & Maryland

Sharpsburg
Frederick
BALTIMORE
Harpers
Ferry
Potomac R.
Winchester
District of
Columbia
Shenandoah Mountains
Shenandoah Valley
Thoroughfare Gap
WASHINGTON
Rectortown
Alexandria
Front Royal
N
Manassas Jct.
Bristoe Sta.
10 Miles
New
Market
Blue Ridge Mtns.
Culpeper
Rappahannock Sta.
Aquia Cr.
Rapidan R.
Falmouth
Chancellorsville
Fredericksburg
Spotsylvania
Potomac R.
Gordonsville
N. Anna R.
Rappahannock R.
Staunton
S. Anna R.
Mattaponi R.
Pamunkey R.
Mechanicsville
Gaines
Mill
Cold
Harbor
Chesapeake Bay
Seven
Pines
York R.
RICHMOND
Chickahominy R.
Appomattox R.
Malvern Hill
Appomattox
C.H.
Harrison's
Landing
Yorktown
Bermuda
Hundred
Williamsburg
PETERSBURG
James R.
Fort Monroe
Norfolk
Gosport Navy
Yard

Civil War Chronology

1860

November 6   Abraham Lincoln is elected president of the United States.

December 20   South Carolina becomes the first state to secede from the Union.

1861

January-April   Mississippi, Florida, Alabama, Georgia, Louisiana, and Texas also secede from the Union.

April 1   Bombardment of Fort Sumter begins the Civil War.

April-May   Lincoln calls for volunteers to fight the Southern rebellion, causing a second wave of secession with Virginia, Arkansas, Tennessee, and North Carolina all leaving the Union.

May   Union naval forces begin blockading the Confederate coast and reoccupying some Southern ports and offshore islands.

July 21   Union forces are defeated at the First Battle of Bull Run and withdraw to Washington.

1862

February   Previously unknown Union general Ulysses S. Grant captures Confederate garrisons in Tennessee at Fort Henry (February 6) and Fort Donelson (February 16).

March 7-8   Confederates and their Cherokee allies are defeated at Pea Ridge, Arkansas.

March 8-9   Naval battle at Hampton Roads, Virginia, involving the USS *Monitor* and the CSS *Virginia* (formerly the USS *Merrimac*) begins the era of the armored fighting ship.

April-July   The Union army marches on Richmond after an amphibious landing. Confederate forces block Northern advance in a series of battles. Robert E. Lee is placed in command of the main Confederate army in Virginia.

April 6-7   Grant defeats the Southern army at Shiloh Church, Tennessee, after a costly two-day battle.

April 27   New Orleans is captured by Union naval forces under Admiral David Farragut.

May 31   The battle of Seven Pines (also called Fair Oaks) is fought and the Union lines are held.

August 29-30   Lee wins substantial victory over the Army of the Potomac at the Second Battle of Bull Run near Manassas, Virginia.

September 17   Union General George B. McClellan repulses Lee's first invasion of the North at Antietam Creek near Sharpsburg, Maryland, in the bloodiest single day of the war.

November 13   Grant begins operations against the key Confederate fortress at Vicksburg, Mississippi.

December 13   Union forces suffer heavy losses storming Confederate positions at Fredericksburg, Virginia.

1863

January 1   President Lincoln issues the Emancipation Proclamation, freeing the slaves in the Southern states.

May 1-6	Lee wins an impressive victory at Chancellorsville, but key Southern commander Thomas J. "Stonewall" Jackson dies of wounds, an irreplaceable loss for the Army of Northern Virginia.
June	The city of Vicksburg and the town of Port Hudson are held under siege by the Union army. They surrender on July 4.
July 1-3	Lee's second invasion of the North is decisively defeated at Gettysburg, Pennsylvania.
July 16	Union forces led by the black 54th Massachusetts Infantry attempt to regain control of Fort Sumter by attacking the Fort Wagner outpost.
September 19-20	Confederate victory at Chickamauga, Georgia, gives some hope to the South after disasters at Gettysburg and Vicksburg.

1864

February 17	A new Confederate submarine, the *Hunley,* attacks and sinks the USS *Housatonic* in the waters off Charleston.
March 9	General Grant is made supreme Union commander. He decides to campaign in the East with the Army of the Potomac while General William T. Sherman carries out a destructive march across the South from the Mississippi to the Atlantic coast.
May-June	In a series of costly battles (Wilderness, Spotsylvania, and Cold Harbor), Grant gradually encircles Lee's troops in the town of Petersburg, Richmond's railway link to the rest of the South.
June 19	The siege of Petersburg begins, lasting for nearly a year until the end of the war.
August 27	General Sherman captures Atlanta and begins the "March to the Sea," a campaign of destruction across Georgia and South Carolina.
November 8	Abraham Lincoln wins reelection, ending hope of the South getting a negotiated settlement.
November 30	Confederate forces are defeated at Franklin, Tennessee, losing five generals. Nashville is soon captured (December 15-16).

1865

April 2	Major Petersburg fortifications fall to the Union, making further resistance by Richmond impossible.
April 3-8	Lee withdraws his army from Richmond and attempts to reach Confederate forces still holding out in North Carolina. Union armies under Grant and Sheridan gradually encircle him.
April 9	Lee surrenders to Grant at Appomattox, Virginia, effectively ending the war.
April 14	Abraham Lincoln is assassinated by John Wilkes Booth, a Southern sympathizer.

Union Army
Army of the Potomac
Army of the James
Army of the Cumberland

Confederate Army
Army of Northern Virginia
Army of Tennessee

A section of the prison camp at Andersonville, Georgia, where prisoners endured unspeakable hardships.

I

Prisoners of Politics

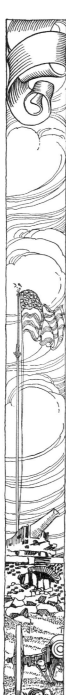

Here, by hundreds, they offered up their lives in their country's cause, victims of disease, starvation, and exposure,—sufferings a thousand times more dreadful than the wounds of the battle-fields.

> —Union Lieutenant Colonel Charles Farnsworth, giving testimony of what he saw at Belle Isle Prison Camp in 1864

"War is cruelty, and you cannot refine it," said Union General William Tecumseh Sherman of the American Civil War.

During the Civil War, which claimed more than 600,000 lives in the North and the South combined, the prisoners of war suffered the most cruelty of all. Nearly 410,000 soldiers became prisoners. Tens of thousands were released by their captors on the battlefield and never saw a prison camp. But thousands were marched to 150 Federal or Confederate prisons and almost 60,000 of them died from disease, starvation, and simple neglect.

Some prisons were nothing more than local county jails where captured soldiers were held in relative

comfort. Other prisons were crumbling warehouses or sprawling, walled stockades where men by the thousands suffered and died. Fifty such large prisons and camps were divided evenly between the North and the South.

At the larger prison camps, the death of one out of every four prisoners was common. In the North, one-quarter of Confederate prisoners at the Elmira, New York, prison camp died—the highest death rate at any Yankee prison camp. In the South, 29 percent of Union prisoners died in Camp Sumter at Andersonville, Georgia; and 34 percent of Union prisoners died in the camp at Salisbury, South Carolina.

When the war began in April 1861, both sides appointed army officers to deal with prisoners of war. The Union selected Colonel William Hoffman to oversee prisons, and the Confederacy selected Brigadier General John H. Winder. During the first year of the war, relatively few prisoners were captured by opposing armies. Most were "paroled" on the battlefield. Parole required that a captured soldier give his word not to take up arms again until he was formally "exchanged" by the governments in Washington and Richmond, Virginia. This simple "gentleman's agreement" proved adequate until the second year of the war. Then, in 1862, battles such as Shiloh in Tennessee and Antietam created prisoners of war by the thousands. The sudden reality of large numbers of captured men required the construction of prison compounds. In these new prison camps, as described by Virginia Polytechnic Institute's Professor James I. Robertson Jr., 125 years later, "Men perished under conditions of filth and terror never known before and not to be equalled until World War II."

Five different kinds of prison compounds were used during the Civil War. A few forts on the Atlantic Coast

were used by both sides for smaller numbers of prisoners. Castle Pinckney in the harbor of Charleston, South Carolina, and Fort Warren in Boston Harbor, Massachusetts are two examples.

As the war continued to produce prisoners, each side converted its own military training and staging campgrounds into prison camps. Examples were Camp Chase in Columbus, Ohio, and Camp Douglas in Chicago, Illinois. Vacant buildings and warehouses became prisons, such as Libby Prison at Richmond, Virginia, and Castle Thunder at Petersburg, Virginia.

When warehouses were full of prisoners of war, tent cities inside tall stockade walls were built, such as the Union's Point Lookout prison camp in Maryland and the Confederacy's Belle Isle camp on the James River near Richmond. And when these camps overflowed with hungry soldiers, stockade camps were hastily

Rebel prisoners were made to march into Union camps on foot.

13

built without any shelters inside for prisoners who froze in the winter and broiled under the summer sun. These open-air encampments of suffering included Camp Salisbury, North Carolina, and the infamous Camp Sumter at Andersonville, Georgia.

During the first two years of the war, both sides tended to parole prisoners of war on the battlefields where they were captured. Although battlefield releases did occur throughout the war, they were greatly reduced during the war's second two years of bloodshed. Between 1861 and the war's end in 1865, the Union forces captured 462,000 Confederate soldiers and sailors. Of these, at least 247,000 were paroled on their pledge to return home and to not rejoin the Confederate army or navy until formally exchanged. Likewise, the Confederates captured 211,000 Yankees and paroled 16,000.

In May 1862 Confederate prisoners who were captured in the Shenandoah Valley are guarded by Union soldiers.

By July 1862 both sides had captured so many thousands of prisoners that the informal gentleman's agreement between opposing armies had to become a formal agreement between the two nations at war. Washington and Richmond agreed to a formula for trading prisoners of war: One Rebel private soldier was equal to one Yankee private soldier. One sergeant would be equal to two privates; one lieutenant would be traded for four privates, and on up to captured generals who would be worth sixty privates. This agreement lasted only one year.

First, on December 28, 1862, President Lincoln's secretary of war, Edwin Stanton, stopped the exchange of Confederate officers. Then, by the spring of 1863, the prisoner exchange agreement collapsed completely over the explosive issue of African American soldiers fighting for the Union.

Until the last months of the war, the Confederacy refused to recognize blacks in the Union army as real soldiers worthy of parole and exchange. Nearly 178,000 Northern blacks and emancipated, Southern slaves served in the United States army and navy. Most served in the units known as the United States Colored Troops under the command of white officers, and they saw action in 449 battles both large and small. Blacks born free in the North were viewed by the Confederacy as Southern slaves. And an army of free African American men wearing Union blue and carrying Springfield or Enfield rifles was the Old South's worst fear for two and a half centuries of slavery. As Professor Joseph T. Glatthaar of the University of Houston, Texas, wrote: "Most Southerners regarded the conduct of Blacks who enlisted in the Union Army as traitorous. . . . Their greatest nightmare was a slave uprising, and in a very real way, Blacks in Union blue were a fulfillment of that horror scenario."

From that fear, Confederate President Jefferson Davis proposed to the Confederate congress on January 12, 1863, that a law should be passed allowing the Confederacy to execute captured Federal officers who commanded free blacks in battle. To the mind of the Old South, arming blacks was the terrifying crime of inciting slave rebellion—a crime punishable by death. The Confederate congress passed such a law in May of 1863. That law contributed much to ending prisoner exchanges for the next two terrible years. As far as the South and the Confederate congress were concerned, every captured African American Yankee would be sold into Southern slavery and his white officers would be killed.

The North was outraged by the Confederate position on enslaving black Union soldiers and executing their white officers. Abraham Lincoln reacted with a furious presidential proclamation, dated July 30, 1863:

> It is the duty of every government to give protection to its citizens, of whatever class, color, or condition, and especially to those who are duly organized as soldiers in the public service. . . . To sell or enslave any captured person, on account of his color, and for no offense against the laws of war, is a relapse into barbarism and a crime against the civilization of the age. . . . It is therefore ordered that for every soldier of the United States killed in violation of the laws of war, a Rebel soldier shall be executed; and for every one enslaved by the enemy or sold into slavery, a Rebel soldier shall be placed at hard labor on the public works and continued at such labor until the other shall be released and receive the treatment due to a prisoner of war.

Prisoners exchanged by the South are returned to Union lines on the USS New York.

The war of words over Confederate treatment of black Federals ended formal exchanges of prisoners. The long-term result was leaving prisoners of war in their miserable prison camps until the war ended. The effect in the South was especially deadly. By the end of 1863, shortages of food and medicine were felt by Confederate armies and by Southern civilians. Unable to exchange tens of thousands of Yankee prisoners of war, food rations in Southern prison camps would be stretched to the limit and beyond. Even Southerners recognized the tragedy of starvation which was about to come to Yankee prisoners. Kate Cumming was a Southern woman and a nurse to wounded Confederate soldiers. She kept a diary of her hospital years, and in it she blamed President Lincoln for the Yankee prisoners dying throughout the hungry South. On December 30, 1863, she wrote in her diary:

> Lincoln has again refused to exchange prisoners. I do think this is the cruelist act of which he has been guilty, not only to us, but his own men . . . [W]e can scarcely get enough of the necessaries of

Three Confederate soldiers captured at Gettysburg await their long march to captivity.

life to feed our own men; and how can he expect us to feed his. . . . [A]ll the prisoners we have might die of starvation.

On April 17, 1864, the feud between the North and the South over black Union soldiers caused Lieutenant General Ulysses S. Grant to declare for the Union government, "No distinction whatever will be made in the exchange between white and colored prisoners." Within four months, General Grant was recommending the total end of prisoner exchanges. On August 19, 1864, he wrote to Union Secretary of State William Seward, "We ought not make a single exchange nor release a prisoner on any pretext whatever until the war closes."

The exchange of prisoners was over, and starving Yankees and Rebels far from home were caught between politics and death in 150 prison camps and old warehouses.

Throughout our bloodied country, a few prisoners of war still managed to be paroled, but most had to wait until the summer of 1865. In cities and small towns, the sad scene witnessed by a Southern woman, Mary Chesnut, would be repeated for two years. Throughout the war, Mrs. Chesnut kept one of the war's most famous and elegant diaries of life in the Confederate States of America. On March 24, 1864, she wrote in her diary about going to the Confederate capitol building in Richmond to welcome home a handful of Rebel prisoners of war:

> Yesterday we went to the capitol grounds to see our returned prisoners . . . . Oh, these men were so forlorn, so dried up, shrunken, such a strange look in some of their eyes. Others, so restless and wild looking—others again, placidly vacant, as if they had been dead to this world for years. A poor woman was too much for me. She was hunting her son. He had been expected back with this batch of prisoners. She said he was taken prisoner at Gettysburg. She kept going in and out among them, with a basket of provisions she had brought for him to eat. It was too pitiful. She was utterly unconscious of the crowd. The anxious dread— expectation—hurry and hope which led her on showed in her face.

The grieving mother did not find her son that day. Perhaps he was rotting in some faraway Yankee prison camp at Elmira, New York, or freezing to death on Lake Erie at Johnson's Island.

Prisoners stand at the deadline—the line that marked
their captivity—enduring the cold and snow of
Johnson's Island.

II

Prisoners of the Yankees

Imagine if you can with the weather ten to fifteen degrees below zero, 100 men trying to keep warm by one stove. Each morning the men crawled out of their bunks shivering and half-frozen, when a scuffle and frequently a fight, for a place by the fire occurred. God help the sick or the weak, as they were literally left out in the cold.

—Rebel soldier, Elmira Prison, New York

A worried Southern father, a Confederate soldier himself, wrote to his wife on July 7, 1863, "I have heard with great grief, my dear Mary, that Fitzhugh has been captured by the enemy." At least the father knew that his captured son was alive when he wrote to his wife on August 2, "I grieve much at his position, but know no way of mending it. . . . I can therefore do nothing but sorrow." By September 10, the father had learned that his prisoner son was wounded but was recovering in the Yankee prison. To his anguished wife he wrote, "Fitzhugh is still a prisoner . . . . His wound is nearly healed and he is able to walk about, though

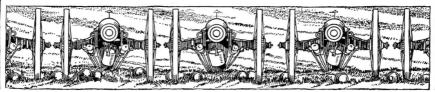

his leg is still stiff." By October 1863 the exchange of prisoners of war had not yet been stopped by the bickering between Washington and Richmond. The father still had hope for his son, Fitzhugh, but he knew better than to ask Yankee officials for help in releasing his wounded son. "I have no idea when Fitzhugh will be exchanged," the weary father wrote to Mary on October 28. "Any desire expressed on our part for an exchange of an individual magnifies the difficulty as they at once think some great benefit is to result to us from it. If you want a person exchanged, the best course is to keep quiet about it." The father concluded, "His detention is very grievous to me."

The Rebel prisoner of war was Fitzhugh Lee. His anxious soldier-father was Robert E. Lee, commanding general of the famed Army of Northern Virginia. The war did not discriminate to whose home it brought grief and worry.

Confederates feared for the safety of their husbands, fathers, and brothers in Federal prison camps. Before prisoner exchanges ended, Southerners saw the wasted condition of the men and boys who were released from Northern prison camps. Occasional truces between the warring countries allowed exchanged prisoners to pass freely through enemy positions. Mothers and wives were horrified at what came home. Confederate nurse, Phoebe Pember, remembered the living skeletons who came home from Northern camps: "Living and dead were taken from the flag-of-truce boat, not distinguishable save from the difference of care exercised in moving them. The Federal prisoners we had released were in many instances in a like state."

During the first two years of the war, the North made every effort to treat Confederate prisoners with care and compassion. General Ulysses S. Grant sent a

letter to Confederate General John C. Pemberton on December 14, 1862, assuring the Rebel general, "All prisoners of war are humanely treated by Federal authorities." But politics, the bitter argument about Southern treatment of captured blacks, and Union outrage over starving Federals in Southern prisons, destroyed much Federal compassion by 1864. In May of that year, Union Secretary of War Edwin Stanton ordered a reduction in food rations to Rebel prisoners in retaliation for the hunger of captured Federals in Confederate prison camps.

For almost 150 years, Americans have charged the Confederacy with starving to death tens of thousands of Federal prisoners of war. They forget the thousands of Confederates who died in filth and squalor in Yankee prisons.

Captured Confederate soldiers await transport to Union prison camps in May 1864.

A Union commission of inquiry, appointed during the war by the United States Sanitary Commission, inspected Federal prison camps and their Confederate prisoners. The inspectors reported: "It is the same story everywhere: prisoners of war treated worse than convicts, shut up either in suffocating buildings, or in outdoor enclosures without even the shelter provided for the beasts of the field; unsupplied with sufficient food; supplied with food and water injurious and even poisonous; compelled to live in such personal uncleanliness as to generate vermin."

The largest Federal prison camp was Point Lookout on the Chesapeake Bay coast of Maryland. Opened in August 1863, a stockade 15 feet high surrounded 40 acres of Confederate prisoners of war. The compound was no more than five feet above sea level. Only Rebel private soldiers were held there, as many as 20,000 men at one time. More than 52,000 Confederates passed through Point Lookout's stockade during the war. There were no buildings to shelter the prisoners from winter cold or summer heat—only shabby tents. When food rations were scarce, prisoners trapped rats to eat. At least 3,000 prisoners died there.

The Northern prison at Alton, Illinois, on the Mississippi River, had the highest death rate of any Yankee prison camp. The prison was built in 1833 as Illinois's first state penitentiary. But the grounds were so swampy and unhealthy that it was closed before the Civil War. The prison reopened for Confederate prisoners of war in February 1862. One year later, a smallpox outbreak at Alton killed 300 men. Between 7,000 and 12,000 Confederates passed through Camp Alton in three years. Of these, 2,218 Confederates died in a prison too dangerous for Illinois to house their convicted criminals there.

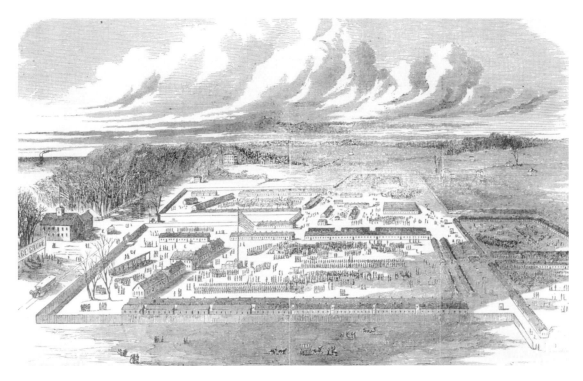

In Chicago, Illinois, Camp Douglas prison was named for Senator Stephen A. Douglas, the man who beat Abraham Lincoln in the United States Senate race of 1858—and the man whom Lincoln beat for the presidency in 1860. When Senator Douglas died in June 1861, the prison camp was erected on land Douglas had owned. In the hard winter of January and February 1863, prisoners died at the rate of 18 every day. During 1863, at least 130 Rebel prisoners died in the camp hospital in one 22-day period. Confederate Private R. T. Bean remembered the scurvy at Camp Douglas: "Lips were eaten away, jaws became diseased, and teeth fell out. If leprosy is any worse than scurvy, may God have mercy upon the victim. It was shocking, horrible, monstrous, and a disgrace to any people who permitted such conditions to exist."

Camp Douglas in Chicago was turned into a prisoner of war camp to house prisoners taken during the campaigns on the Mississippi River and its tributaries.

Prisoners being held at Camp Douglas were featured in the Harper's Weekly *of April 5, 1862. They had been captured at the battle for Fort Donelson.*

The prison compound at Camp Douglas consisted of about 20 acres with 64 barracks. Each barracks was set up to hold about 95 men but would eventually hold almost 190. When the first Confederate prisoners arrived in February 1862, no provisions had been made to supply food, clothing, or medical care.

Guards at the Chicago camp outlined a "deadline" along the fence of the camp to prevent escape attempts. The deadline was a railing or a series of stakes along the inside perimeter of the camp about 10 feet from the exterior wall. If a prisoner crossed this line, he would be immediately killed by the guards. One of the commanders at Camp Douglas punished the camp for an attempted escape by moving the deadline further in so the prisoners were confined to an even smaller area.

Punishment of prisoners for minor infractions was severe. Men were locked in rooms only eight feet square and seven feet high for days, with only two holes for air. Cannonballs weighing almost 32 pounds were attached to many mens' legs by chains for minor infractions. The men started calling these their "time-pieces."

In May of 1864, when Colonel Benjamin Sweet became commandant of Camp Douglas, he seemed more concerned about the lack of security than the appalling conditions inside the camp. He added a 12-foot-high fence around the perimeter of the two fences already in place. An elevated walkway was put on top of the fence so the guards would have a better view of the entire grounds. To prevent tunneling as a means of escape, he had all of the barracks raised on four-foot posts. Colonel Sweet forbade the use of candles, and prisoners were required to go to bed at sundown and stay there until a bugle sounded at daybreak. No talking was allowed in the barracks at night under threat of being shot through the wall if the guards heard the sound of voices.

The main causes of death at Camp Douglas were typhoid fever and pneumonia from the poor sanitary conditions and exposure to the extreme weather. A smallpox epidemic killed many of the prisoners. As Confederate Private T. M. Page remembered it, "To the helpless agony of this situation, smallpox added its own horror."

An inspector from the Sanitary Commission found the Camp Douglas barracks to be in poor condition and reported that "all of the prisoners' barracks are greatly in need of repair. There is not a door and hardly a window among them; a large proportion of the bunks are so mutilated as to be useless; much of the flooring and siding is removed and the open fire-

"The prisoners were poorly fed, worse bedded, and nearly suffocated in the impure air. It is said there have been as many as 1,700 men at one time in these lower quarters. That number could scarcely find standing room; sleeping would be out of the question; of course they must suffer, sicken, and die."—Griffin Frost, prisoner at Old Capitol Prison (right) Washington, D.C.

places in the cook houses are in a dilapidated condition; the roofs of all require repairs."

Some of the people of Chicago sought to aid the men in the camp with donations of food and clothing. But soon the compassionate citizens were forbidden to bring their assistance to the Confederate prisoners.

Camp conditions and Confederate courage inspired at least one escape attempt. At 10:00 on the night of September 27, 1864, all was quiet throughout Camp Douglas when 30 prisoners charged out of their barracks and ran for the northwest corner of the compound. The man in the lead hastily threw a blanket over the lantern at the fence. The guard, alerted by the sudden darkness, shot in the direction of the light, wounding the prisoner in the face. The 29 other Rebels were not deterred. Using axes and hammers, they beat down part of the fence. Gunfire from guards aiming into the dark corner drove the prisoners back into their barracks. No one had made it to freedom and 12 daring prisoners were put in ball and chains by the morning.

Camp Douglas housed 12,000 Confederate prisoners of war by December 1864. More than 18,000 prisoners passed through its gates during the war. When Yankee doctors inspected Camp Douglas, they reported, "Filth, poor drainage, and overcrowding created a horror."

The other large prison camp in Illinois was Rock Island, described by Federal doctors as a camp suffering from "a striking want of some means for the preservation of human life." The first Confederate prisoners arrived at Rock Island on December 3, 1863. Although the first group of prisoners numbered only 468, by the end of December, 98 were dead from smallpox. By the end of the war, at least 1,800 Confederates had died from smallpox at Rock Island. Six thousand prisoners were crammed into the camp by January 1864. Just in that month, 231 prisoners died from filth and disease. In February another 350 died. By July 1864, 1,300 prisoners had died in seven months. Of the

The peaceful scene of the Johnson's Island prison camp below belies the horror of being incarcerated there.

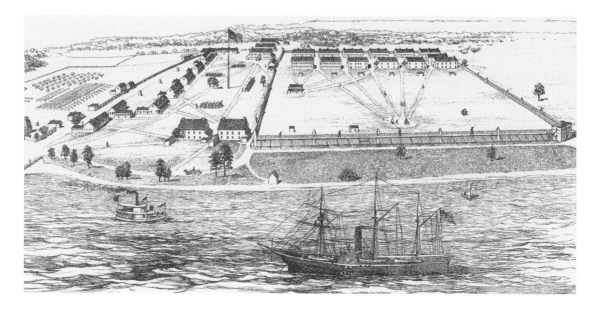

Confederate General John Hunt Morgan made a successful escape from an Ohio prison in 1863.

12,000 Confederates who passed through Rock Island, at least 1,950 died there.

Johnson's Island prison camp was especially feared by Southerners. Holding only Confederate officers, the island is three miles from Sandusky, Ohio, on Lake Erie. Winters were especially hard on men born and raised in a warm climate. From April 1862 through September 1865, more than 9,000 Rebel officers were held on the island inside its 16-acre compound. Twelve wooden barracks offered some shelter from the cold, but 300 men died there. Many trapped and ate rats when food rations were small. Seven Confederate generals were imprisoned on the island by the end of the war.

The Ohio State Penitentiary in Columbus, Ohio, was turned into a military prison in 1862. It was chosen as the prison for the notorious Confederate general, John Hunt Morgan, and 30 of his men, because of its additional security. But Morgan and six of his men thwarted that security, dug through the stone floor with kitchen knives, crawled through an air shaft, and made one of the most famous escapes from a Northern prison.

Fifteen thousand Confederate prisoners passed through Camp Morton prison compound near Indianapolis, Indiana. In three years over 1,700 men died there. Before the war, the prison camp had been the home of the Indiana State Fair.

The most infamous Yankee prison was at Elmira, New York, where many Confederates saw their first

ice storms and snowdrifts. Ten thousand Rebel prisoners lived on 40 acres. Elmira began as a Northern training camp which served 21,000 Yankees going to war. It became a prison in July 1864 and remained open for a year. Thirty-five buildings stood inside a stockade wall 12-feet high. Official estimates reported that only 5,000 men could live in the camp. But by the end of its first month, more than 4,400 Confederates were imprisoned there. By the second month, there were 9,600 prisoners. Eight hundred of them already had scurvy from poor diets. Teeth and hair were falling out of the scurvy patients. By September 1864 more than 1,870 prisoners suffered from scurvy. The citizens of Elmira paid 10 cents each to climb an observation tower near the prison to see the starving, sickly Confederates.

Elmira prison camp was in New York, where the winters were especially cold and harsh for Southern prisoners.

The tedium and loneliness of life in prison took its toll on the minds and bodies of the soldiers.

The source of most of the disease at Elmira was Foster's Pond, a stagnant puddle 40 feet wide in the middle of camp. Human waste and garbage filled the pond. Just its smell made men vomit. By October 1864 five prisoners every day were dying of disease. By December smallpox raced through the camp.

Confederate prisoner Private Walter D. Addison remembered Elmira's doctors 25 years later: "If they had been dumb brutes, instead of human beings as they were supposed to be, they could not have exhibited greater brutality."

When prisoners' conduct resulted in punishment, they were often confined in Elmira's "sweat box," which was little more than a coffin stood on its end. The sweat box was 7 feet tall, 20 inches wide, and 12 inches deep. A man locked inside could not move his arms. Only the air holes prevented death from suffocation. Private Addison remembered the sweat box well: "For trivial offenses, our men were therein confined for hours in the scorching suns of July and August, without food and water, and removed in many cases only when the victim was more dead than alive. I vividly recollect when one man dropped with rigid limbs swollen and almost paralyzed, and died in a few days from the effects."

One-fourth of Elmira's prisoners died there. With 2,963 dead out of 12,123 prisoners, Elmira had the second highest death rate of any Yankee prison camp. Of these dead, 1,233 were from North Carolina, 387 were from South Carolina, and 550 were from Virginia.

The national cemetery at Andersonville, Georgia.

III

Prisoners of the Rebels

Many came in who had been in good health during their service in the field but who seem utterly overwhelmed by the appalling misery they saw on every hand, and giving away to despondency, died in a few days or weeks.
—Private John McElroy, Andersonville

Salisbury prison camp at Salisbury, North Carolina, was that state's only Civil War prison. Covering 16 acres inside a wooden stockade, the first captured Federals arrived in December 1861. Within the stockade were a few small buildings and one, four-story factory used for processing cotton before the war. With room for only 2,000 prisoners, the compound was crowded with more than 10,000 Federals by October 1864. By April 1865, at least 3,400 prisoners had died from starvation and disease.

In South Carolina, Yankee prisoners suffered inside the stockade camp at Florence. The camp was built by 1,000 slaves who finished their work in the fall of 1864. On 23 acres inside a stockade wall 12 feet high,

Castle Thunder was one of the major Confederate prisons in Richmond, Virginia.

between 15,000 and 18,000 Federal prisoners of war passed through the camp. By October 1864 the camp contained 12,362 prisoners who were dying at the rate of 25 every day. During its brief operation of only five months, more than 2,800 prisoners died.

Richmond, Virginia, the Confederate capital city, had two major prison compounds, Libby Prison and Castle Thunder. (Another Castle Thunder prison was located at Petersburg, Virginia.) The Richmond Castle Thunder was generally reserved for political prisoners. Federal officers were held at Libby Prison.

A four-story factory owned by shipbuilders marked the center of Libby Prison. The factory became barracks for Yankee officers. When disease at Libby Prison overwhelmed the prison hospital tents, sick prisoners were taken to Richmond's three prison hospitals. The three hospitals had 500 beds between them. But by the middle of March 1864, they were treating more than 1,100 Yankee patients.

The first prisoners arrived at Libby in March 1862. At first, the prison conditions were not as difficult as most. But conditions at Libby deteriorated rapidly when prisoner exchanges with the North all but stopped in the summer of 1863. By winter the prison was overcrowded and new captives arrived daily. Eventually, the Libby Prison population increased to over 1,200 men on each floor. The rooms became filthy with the excrement of men not allowed to use the latrine at night when they suffered from diarrhea and vomiting. Floors became caked with filth. Lice, fleas, bedbugs, and flies plagued the prisoners. The over-crowding became such a problem that at night the prisoners were unable to turn over as they were forced to lay on their sides against each other "spoon style." Soon not everyone could lay down at the same time. Some men stood while others slept.

Lack of food was worse than the lack of sleep. Union General Neal Dow wrote in his Libby Prison diary on February 22, 1864: "There have been issued to us yesterday and today, instead of meat, about 1 gill (about 4 ounces) each, of a very small bean, called 'cow pea' in the south. They are very poor at best, but these are old and full of worms—worthless."

Orders were given in early March 1864 that no prisoner could look out a window or he would be shot. On May 6 General Dow wrote: "Some of the guards, not all, are longing to shoot any one who looks out of the window. All the windows are barred with iron. This morning some officers were standing near, not at a window, when a sentinel drew up his gun quickly and snapped at them." Other prisoners were not so lucky. Prisoner Joseph Grider remembered, "They would not let you look out the windows. They shot seven men looking out; one was shot on my floor . . . [H]e had just put his hand out to throw out some water."

Filth, hunger, and trigger-happy guards at Libby Prison inspired one of the war's most daring prison

The interior of Libby prison as depicted in Harper's Weekly *in October of 1863. (The name of the prison was spelled a number of different ways.)*

escapes. Yankee Major Andrew G. Hamilton designed a plan to tunnel down to the basement of the four-story building, then down through the basement floor, under the street, and up to freedom—in the middle of the capital city of the Confederate States of America. He enlisted the help of 25 other prisoners. Colonel Thomas E. Rose took command of the project and the 25 men took turns in shifts of 7 or 8 with the digging.

The tunnel began behind one of the stoves on the second floor. The men went through the wall and down inside the wall to the basement. There was an area of the basement covered with straw. Under the straw, the Federal prisoners dug down almost nine feet. They tunneled across and under the basement, under the street, under a shed on the other side, and then upward. "The work was all accomplished secretly at night . . . [T]wo men, having quietly removed the bricks, would go down and take turns digging throughout the night," explained James Wells, one of the prisoners involved in the escape. Other prisoners would haul out the dirt, spread it on the basement floor, and cover it with the straw so it would not be detected. In 47 days, the dangerous project was completed.

On February 9, 1864, the 25 men who had labored so hard were the first to crawl through the tunnel to the outside. Only then were others in the prison told of the tunnel. In all, 109 Union officers crawled underground, on their hands and knees into Richmond. Once on the outside, they separated into small groups, all going by a different route north toward Federal lines.

The exterior of Libby Prison in Richmond, Virginia, where Union officers were held after their capture.

Soldiers in captivity often wrote on the walls of the prison and sometimes would be shot for looking out of a window.

In the morning at roll call, the Confederate guards found a large number of prisoners missing but could find no means of escape. It would be hours before one of the guards discovered the tunnel under the basement straw.

Of the 109 men who had crawled through the tunnel, 48 were recaptured by the pursuing Rebels, 2 drowned in an attempt to swim across the James River, and 59 reached the safety of the Union lines.

Near Richmond within view of Libby Prison, Belle Isle prison camp stood on an island in the James River. Between 7,000 and 10,000 Federals were held on the island at one time.

Belle Isle was originally set up to hold about 3,000 prisoners. But the end of prisoner exchanges quickly filled Belle Isle beyond its limit for humane treatment. With more prisoners than double its capacity, many prisoners were forced to sleep outside on unprotected ground. Many dug holes in which to sleep. Those prisoners in tents did not fare much better. The tents were ragged, full of holes, and more than 12 men squeezed into each small tent.

Lieutenant Colonel Charles Farnsworth, a Union officer held in Libby Prison, was allowed to go to Belle Isle to help distribute some clothing sent by the United States Sanitary Commission. He wrote this account in his journal:

> [T]he part occupied by the prisoners is low, sandy, barren waste, exposed in summer to a burning sun, without the shadow of a single tree; and in winter, to the damp and cold winds up the river, with a few miserable tents, in which, perhaps, one-half the number were protected from the night fogs of a malarious region; the others lay upon the ground in the open air. One of them said to me: 'We lay in rows, like hogs in winter, and take turns who has the outside of the row.'

Five hospital tents were set up outside of the prisoner area—just north of them was the graveyard. The

The conditions on Belle Isle were so horrific it was finally evacuated—but the prisoners were taken to Andersonville, where conditions were even worse.

hospital tents had no flooring and only straw covered the ground. Logs were placed among the straw to serve as pillows for the sick and dying.

The winter of 1863-64 was especially cold and the Yankee prisoners on Belle Isle suffered greatly. Private George Dingman testified to the terrible conditions: "[T] he men would run all night to keep warm, and in the morning I would see men lying dead; from three to six to seven; they were frozen; this was nearly every morning I was there."

When the Belle Isle survivors were released, more than 90 percent of the emaciated prisoners weighed less than 100 pounds. Union prisoner, Private William D. Foote, remembered the starvation on Belle Island: "There was no name for our hunger. When a bone would be thrown away by some, it would be taken up often by others, and boiled to get something out of it."

Doctors examine an emaciated soldier after he was released from the prison camp on Belle Isle.

When poet Walt Whitman first saw newly released prisoners from Belle Isle, he said, "Can these be men? . . . [A]re they not mummied, dwindled corpses? They lay there, most of them, quite still, but with a horrible look in their eyes."

Of all prison camps, whether in the North or the South, none is associated with as much horror as Camp Sumter at Andersonville, Georgia. The camp is remembered simply as Andersonville.

Andersonville opened in February 1864. Within one month, 7,500 captured Federals were held within 26

acres surrounded by a stockade wall. By May there were 15,000 men. And by August 1864 more than 33,000 prisoners were starving and dying. There were no buildings to protect them from wind and weather. Even tents were rare. Men lived in the mud and filth outside. The Confederacy could provide only 13 doctors for 33,000 prisoners. In March 1865, weeks before the war ended, one Rebel medical assistant said of Andersonville's chief surgeon, Dr. R. Randolph Stevenson: ". . . a poor medical man and no surgeon, but an energetic officer in trying to provide for the wants and comforts of the sick."

When Andersonville's prison population reached 33,000 in the summer of 1864, the prison camp became the fifth largest city in the entire South. At the same time, prisoners were dying at the rate of more than 100 every day. During its little more than one year in operation, the camp's death rate averaged 90 to 130 dead

A view of Andersonville prison showing the deadline set up to keep men away from the wall.

These four sketches were in Harper's Weekly *of September 1865 showing some of the torture Union prisoners endured at Andersonville.*

Federals per day. Many died from starvation. Prisoner Private John McElroy remembered, "[I]t was very hard work to banish thoughts and longings for food from out minds. Hundreds actually became insane brooding over it. . . . We thought of food all day and were visited with torturing dreams of it at night."

In May 1864 a Catholic priest, Reverend William John Hamilton, came to the camp to minister to those of his faith. He saw the need of all who were there. He petitioned his bishop for assistance in ministering to the prisoners. Father Hamilton, Father Claveril, and Father Whelan came everyday to talk with the prisoners, to hear their confessions, and to bless them before dying, sometimes laying down beside them in comfort as they took their last breath. Some prisoners of other faiths began holding prayer services on their own and large crowds would join them when they heard the strains of familiar hymns through the haze of their misery.

Religious comfort did not ease the daily grim reality of Andersonville. The camp commandant, Captain Henry Wirz, established a deadline on the inside of the stockade walls. The imaginary line marked by sticks and rags was 13 feet within the walls. Any prisoner who crossed over the deadline was shot and killed by guards. Many men who could no longer stand the suffering crossed the line to commit suicide. Starvation and disease turned prisoners of war into wild animals who preyed upon each other. Men stole food from the mouths of dying friends or stripped the rags of clothing from dead bodies. Violence among the prisoners became so ferocious that Captain Wirz allowed the Yankee prisoners to police their own thieves and cutthroats. On July 12, 1864, while Confederate guards watched, the prisoners of Andersonville hanged six of their own men to stop the violence. Another three men were beaten to death.

BALL & CHAIN.

SHOT ON THE DEAD LINE FOR A PIECE OF MOULDY CAKE.

One month after the Andersonville lynchings, the prisoners witnessed Camp Sumter's one and only miracle: After a heavy Georgia rainstorm, a fresh spring of water opened just inside the deadline by the west wall. Thirsty, starving prisoners called it Providence Spring. Private McElroy wrote in his memoirs:

One morning the camp was astonished beyond measure to discover that during the night a large bold spring had burst out on the north side, about midway between the swamp and the summit of

This Civil War song was composed in 1864 by George F. Root. He wanted to put hope into the hearts of those waiting for prisoners of war to be released.

Tramp! Tramp! Tramp!

In the prison cell I sit
Thinking Mother dear, of you,
And our bright and happy home so far away,
And the tears they fill my eyes
'Spite of all that I can do
Tho' I try to cheer my comrades and be gay.

Chorus
Tramp, tramp, tramp, the boys are marching,
Cheer up, comrades, they will come
And beneath the starry flag
We shall breath the air again,
Of the free-land in our own beloved home.

In the battle front we stood
When their fiercest charge they made,
And they swept us off, a hundred men or more,
But before we reached their lines,
They were beaten back dismayed,
And we heard the cry of victory o'er and o'er.
Chorus

So within the prison cell
We are waiting for the day,
That shall come to open wide the iron door,
And the hollow eyes grow bright,
And the poor heart almost gay,
As we think of seeing home and friends once more.
Chorus

the hill. It poured out its grateful flood of pure sweet water in an apparently exhaustless quantity. To the many who looked in wonder upon it, it seemed as truly heaven-wrought. . . . The police took charge of the spring and everyone was compelled to take his regular turn in filling his vessel. This was kept up during our whole stay in Andersonville.

Writing about Andersonville in 1988, Princeton University's Professor Reid Mitchell said, "Andersonville became a pit of depravity." In that pit of depravity and hunger, at least 13,000 Federal prisoners died. When the war was over, Captain Wirz would pay for those deaths with his own life.

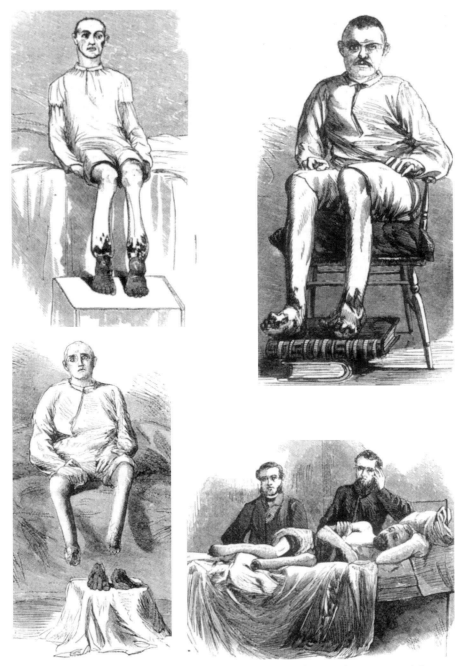

Sketches of the pain and suffering endured by those who returned from Confederate prison camps.

IV

Death by Rope and by Fire

From my experience of fifteen years of constant medical and military service . . . I affirm that the treatment to which our men have been subjected while prisoners of war in the hands of the enemy, is against all rules of civilized warfare . . . where the lives and comfort of prisoners of war is a matter of such cruel indifference, to say the least, if not indeed, as one might almost be justified in supposing, a matter of determined policy.

—B. A. VanderKrieft, surgeon in the
United States Army, May 31, 1864

When the grim national tragedy was over in 1865, at least 660,000 men in the North and the South were dead. Many of them died in prison camps. Almost 215,000 Confederate prisoners of war were held in Yankee prisons. Of them, at least 26,000 died from disease, exposure to harsh weather, hunger, or poor medical treatment.

Nearly 195,000 Federal prisoners of war were held in Southern prisons. More than 30,000 died. Nearly half of them had died at Andersonville. The death rates at all prisons inspired Professor Reid Mitchell to write,

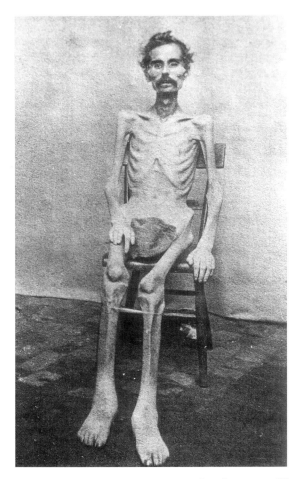

One of the Union soldiers released from a Southern prison.

"The death rate of military prisoners during the Civil War was so high that being in prison was as deadly as being in battle."

In war the victor writes the history. After the Civil War the victorious Northerners needed someone to punish for the 30,000 dead men in Rebel prisons. The government chose Captain Henry Wirz from Camp Sumter, Andersonville.

During the war many prisoner of war camps were managed by "enemy" officers who were actually respected and even admired by their prisoners. Such camp commandants who won their prisoners' affection included Yankee Colonels Charles W. Hill at Johnson's Island and Richard D. Owen at Camp Morton, Indianapolis. The same respect was given to Confederate Lieutenant Colonel Robert C. Smith at the prison camp at Danville, Virginia.

Andersonville and its atrocities at the deadline and within the prisoner population made Captain Henry Wirz a special case.

President Lincoln's Secretary of War, Edwin Stanton, spoke for the North when he said, "There appeared to have been a deliberate system of savage and barbarous treatment and starvation."

It did not help Captain Wirz that he was not a native-born American. His real name was Heinrich Wirz and he was born in Switzerland. He came to the United States in 1849. He served in the Confederate army and his arm was badly wounded in May

1862. He became Andersonville's only commanding officer.

Captain Wirz was arrested in May 1865 and was charged with what today would be called war crimes. He was not tried by a civilian court. Instead, in clear violation of the United States Constitution, he was tried by a military commission. United States Army officers were his judge and jury. His trial began in late August 1865, and it lasted three months.

The tone and language of the military court's formal charges against Captain Wirz expressed the passion of his day. He was charged with "maliciously, willfully, and traitorously . . . conspiring . . . to injure the health and destroy the lives of soldiers in the military service of the United States." He was further charged with "subjecting to torture and great suffering by confining in unhealthy and unwholesome quarters . . . by furnishing insufficient and unwholesome food" the prisoners of war at Andersonville. His character and state of mind where called "his evil design" and his "evil intent." The court accused Captain Wirz of "pursuing his wicked and cruel purpose" by subjecting his pris-

Captain Wirz is depicted committing one of the crimes against Union prisoners for which he was eventually hung.

The execution of Captain Wirz for the atrocities at Andersonville.

oners to "cruel, unusual, and infamous punishment." The court charged the captain with being responsible for the deaths of at least 300 prisoners who were shot after crossing the deadline. He was accused of having used dogs to hunt down and injure or kill at least 50 men who had tried to escape. The court charged that on one occasion, Captain Wirz used "bloodthirsty animals, called bloodhounds, to pursue, attack, wound, and tear in pieces a soldier belonging to the Army of the United States."

Captain Wirz was also accused of killing at least four prisoners with his own hands, three by shooting and one by kicking the prisoner to death.

There is no question that 13,000 men died under his command from unspeakable suffering and deprivation. But historians still argue about how much control Captain Wirz really had over his prison at a time when Southern soldiers and civilians were also going hungry. The political aspect of the trial is revealed in the fact that Captain Wirz was offered a secret "deal": he could save his own life by admitting publicly that Confederate President Jefferson Davis was really behind the systematic starvation of Federal prisoners of war. In a flash of courage and decency—perhaps his only such moment—Captain Wirz refused to blame Davis for Andersonville's horror.

On November 6, 1865, the military court found Captain Wirz guilty of most of the charges and sentenced him to hang. There would be no appeal to any civilian court. Three days later President Andrew Johnson signed the death warrant for Captain Wirz, and he was hanged in Washington on November 10.

The Supreme Court of the United States now stands on the spot where Captain Wirz was hanged in 1865.

Civil War prisoners of war did not only die in filthy prison camps. Some died going to prison and some died coming home.

Weakened by wounds or disease before they were captured, many soldiers did not live long enough to see a prison camp. Hundreds died on the long marches to prisons. Captain Willard W. Glazier recalled of his capture:

On the morning of the twentieth, before sunrise we started for Culpeper. This was one of the severest tramps of my life. The weather was exceedingly warm, and the distance about thirty miles. Our guards were mounted, and evinced but little sympathy with us in our unfortunate condition, as we endeavored to keep pace with them. . . . Curses and threats long and loud were freely indulged in by the guards, because we could not walk even faster than their horses. Before reaching Culpeper six of our number fell by the wayside utterly exhausted.

Most of the soldiers who were captured had their belongings taken from them by their captors, who were in great need of the supplies. But this made the long journeys to the prison camps even more torturous. George Putnam of the 176th New York Volunteers recalled his capture with these words: "They took possession of overcoats, blankets, and the contents of our pockets. They also took what under the circumstance was the most serious loss for men who had a long march before them, our shoes."

Prisoners released by the South received new clothing from the Union army to replace the rags they were wearing.

Other soldiers died while sitting quietly. On July 16, 1864, a prison train full of Confederates steamed through northeast Pennsylvania on the way to infamous Elmira Prison. Near Shohola, Pike County, Pennsylvania, the train crashed, killing 48 Confederate prisoners and 17 Yankee guards.

There were those who didn't survive their train rides to prison not because of a crash, but because of the conditions on the train. "We were taken from Atlanta in open box cars, without shelter; we lay on the floor wounded men and all; men with diarrhea had no accommodations . . . all were packed closely; there were about fifty wounded; some amputations," stated Captain A. R. Calhoun from Kentucky.

For those who survived the prison camps, lived through the horror, deprivation, and illnesses, the long journey home would be a difficult one. Many only survived a few days of freedom before they died. Many spent long weeks or months in military hospitals before they could begin their journey.

One disaster involving returning prisoners towers above all the rest—the wreck of the *Sultana*.

General Robert E. Lee surrendered the shattered remnant of the Army of Northern Virginia on April 9, 1865. Six days later, Abraham Lincoln was assassinated. In the deep South and West, the last Confederate commands would lay down their weapons through April and May. The war was over.

On April 21, 1865, the 1,719-ton paddle-wheel steamboat *Sultana* left New Orleans to follow the Mississippi River northward. Two hundred sixty feet long, the *Sultana* chugged upriver to Vicksburg, Mississippi, which General Grant had captured on the Fourth of July 1863. Now teaming with blue-coated Yankees, Vicksburg was full of newly released Union prisoners from Confederate prison camps. Hundreds were skin-and-bone survivors of Andersonville. Everyone had the same dream—to go home.

The *Sultana* was legally certified to carry only 376 passengers and crewmen. But at Vicksburg, nearly 2,300 former prisoners of war swarmed and hobbled onto the small riverboat. They filled every inch of cabin and deck space. When coffins were loaded on board with the remains of dead soldiers, the former prisoners used the wooden boxes as their beds on deck—anything to get on a boat headed north.

At the Vicksburg dock, workers repaired the *Sultana*'s steam boilers. The *Sultana* reached Memphis, Tennessee, on April 26. Her steam boilers were still leaking, so other workmen at Memphis repaired them as best they could while 2,300 veterans joked and laughed about home cooking—for many their first in four terrible years.

When the boiler repairs were finally completed for the second time in two days, the *Sultana* left the dock near midnight. Two thousand men on deck looked into the darkness, watching for their destination: Cairo, Illinois.

The severely overloaded steamboat swished her way past Memphis. Two hours upriver, only 10 miles north of Memphis, the failing boilers exploded.

At 2:00 in the morning, April 27, the *Sultana* erupted in a cloud of scalding steam and flames. Hundreds of men were boiled alive where they slept. Hundreds were blown into the jet black Mississippi River. As the ship burned the steamboat drifted aimlessly until her smoldering wreck beached briefly on a tiny island. Survivors clinging to the hulk jumped for dry land. More than 600 men still struggled in the water as the current carried them downriver toward Memphis.

Forty-three years later, Private James R. Collins of the 3rd Tennessee Cavalry remembered what he saw and felt when the *Sultana* exploded under his feet: "Men lay everywhere scalded to death by the hot, hissing steam that came from the exploded boilers. Some were killed outright by being struck by falling timbers; others met death from the shock of the explosion, and everywhere on the ill-fated boat, death was visible in countless horrible and shocking forms." Among the men who died that fiery night was Private Collins' father, Joseph H. Collins, also a private in the 3rd Tennessee Cavalry.

Six hundred survivors floated down to Memphis, where they were rescued. Two hundred of them died in Memphis hospitals.

The Sultana's *steam boilers exploded, killing hundreds of released Union soldiers before they could reach their homes again.*

TESTIMONY OF DR. DEWITT C. PETERS, an assistant surgeon in the United States Army, before a committee of the United States Sanitary Commission. Although it describes the condition of some men who were released from Belle Isle, it could be a description of soldiers who had been held at Andersonville, Elmira, Johnson's Island, Libby . . . :

> I am an Assistant Surgeon of the United States Army, stationed at Jarvis General Hospital, Baltimore. On or about the 16th of April, 1864, I received at the hospital over which I have charge, some two hundred and fifty paroled prisoners of war, recently returned from Belle Island and Richmond.
>
> The greater majority of these men were in a semi-state of nudity. They were laboring under such diseases as chronic diarrhea, phthisis pulmonalis, scurvy, frost bites, general debility, caused by starvation, neglect, and exposure.
>
> Many of them had partially lost their reason, forgetting even the date of their capture and everything connected with their antecedent history. They resemble, in many respects, patients laboring under cretinism.
>
> They were filthy in the extreme, covered with vermin. Some had extensive bed sores caused by laying in the sand and dirt, and nearly all were extremely emaciated; so much so that they had to be cared for even like infants.
>
> Their hair had not been cut, nor the men shaved in many instances for months.
>
> On inquiry of these men as to what was the matter with them, the invariable answer was, starvation, exposure, and neglect, while prisoners on Belle Island. . . .
>
> Out of the two hundred and fifty men received by me, so far, fifteen have died; the post-mortems of which have made apparent diseases of nearly all the viscera to a remarkable extent.
>
> I received one man incurably insane, caused, as I was informed and believe, by joy, produced by the news that he was to be exchanged. I found . . . they had become like savages in their habits, and lost the decencies of life, and had to be taught like children the decencies of society.
>
> The health and constitutions of the majority of these men are permanently undermined. . . . I think nine-tenths of the men weighed under one hundred pounds; they appeared to be articulated skeletons . . . and were the most pitiable objects to behold.

When the bodies were counted and the missing men were accounted for by their friends who knew them on board, at least 1,700 people were known dead. The loss of the *Sultana* was the worst loss of life on water by the United States before or since 1865. For 1,700 dead heroes, there was no escape from Confederate prison camps.

Finally those who managed to hold on through it all went home. Many mere skeletons of the soldiers who had marched to the recruiters' drums, maimed in body and mind. Most would spend long months, even years, recovering their health, if they recovered it at all. And as they recovered in body they tried to recover in mind and not let the memory of man's inhumanity rule their hearts and lives. General Sherman was right: "War is cruelty, and you cannot refine it."

Glossary

ball and chain	A 32-pound cannonball attached to a large metal chain, locked onto the leg of a prisoner as punishment and to prevent escape.
bluecoats	Term used for soldiers in the Northern Union army during the Civil War because of the color of their uniforms.
Confederacy	The Confederate States of America; the South.
Confederate	Citizen of the Confederate States of America; a Southerner during the Civil War.
deadline	A line designated inside the perimeter of a prison, usually marked by stakes or a railing, across which prisoners may not cross under penalty of immediate execution.
Federals	A name used for members of the Union.
graycoats	Term used for soldiers in the Southern Confederate army during the Civil War because of the color of their uniforms.
parole	The release of a prisoner of war with the agreement that he will leave the army and return home.
prisoner exchange	Agreement between two sides at war to exchange an equal number of prisoners taken by each side.
Rebels	Term used for Southerners in the Civil War.
scurvy	A disease caused by the lack of vitamin C. It spread through the prison camps because of the lack of fruits and vegetables.
secessionist	Southerners who voted to secede from the Union and form their own republic.

smallpox	A contagious disease usually spread in unsanitary conditions characterized by inflammation of the skin with pustules.
stockade	An area enclosed by a tall solid fence.
typhoid fever	A contagious disease that involves high fever, headache, diarrhea, and inflammation of the intestines.
Union	The United States of America; the North.
United States Sanitary Commission	A Federal commission set up by the secretary of war in 1861 to oversee army hospitals after many women protested the conditions there.
Yankees	Term used for Northerners.

Further Reading

Faust, Patricia L., ed. *Historical Times Illustrated Encyclopedia of the Civil War*. New York: Historical Times, 1986.

Hasseltine, William B., ed., *Civil War Prisons*. Ohio: Kent State University Press, 1962.

Leckie, Robert. *None Died in Vain*. New York: HarperCollins, 1990.

Lee, Ken and Gene Shields. "James R. Collins Describes his Civil War Experiences." Plainsville, KS: *The Plainsville Times*, 28 May 1908.

Levy, George. *To Die in Chicago: Confederate Prisoners at Camp Douglas, 1862-1865*. Louisiana: Pelican Publishing, 1999.

McElroy, John. *This Was Andersonville*. New York: McDowell, Obolensky, 1957.

McPherson, James M. *Battle Cry of Freedom*. New York: Oxford University Press, 1988.

Speer, Lonnie R. *Portals to Hell: Military Prisons of the Civil War*. Pennsylvania: Stackpole Books, 1997.

Websites on Prison Camps in the Civil War

Brothers Bound:
    http://homepages.rootsweb.com/~south1/bound.htm
The Prisons both Union and Confederate:
    http://homepages.rootsweb.com/~south1/prisons.htm

Index

PHOTO CREDITS
Harper's Weekly: pp. 13, 17, 20, 25, 26, 29, 30, 31, 32, 34, 36, 38, 40, 41, 44, 48, 51, 52, 54, 57; Library of Congress: p. 39; National Archives: pp. 14, 18, 28; United States Army Military History Institute: pp. 10, 23, 42, 43, 50